MW01594874

THE CHRISTIAN RESPONSE TO HUNGER IN AMERICA

BARBARA MUSE M.DIV.

WESTBOW
PRESS®

A DIVISION OF THOMAS NELSON
& ZONDERVAN

WestBow Press books may be ordered through booksellers or by contacting:

WestBow Press
A Division of Thomas Nelson & Zondervan
1663 Liberty Drive
Bloomington, IN 47403
www.westbowpress.com
1 (866) 928-1240

ISBN: 978-1-9736-6951-7 (sc)
ISBN: 978-1-9736-6950-0 (e)

Print information available on the last page.

WestBow Press rev. date: 08/05/2019

CONTENTS

FOREWORD

In 2009, my husband Ray and I launched a summer food program as a community outreach effort for our church Bread of Life Development (BOLD) Ministries. We received approval from the State of Georgia to become an Administrative Sponsor of the Summer Food Service Program (SFSP). The SFSP is a United States Department of Agriculture (USDA) funded program, which provides reimbursement to Sponsors who provide free creditable meals to children eighteen and under. The meals we serve must meet the USDA meal pattern requirements for children. The meals include items from five different food groups to help children receive a nutritious balanced meal.

This was a very important outreach project for our ministry to take on. Most of the children that attended our church came from low-income families. Every Sunday during children's church, the children would not even settle down until I could find something for them to eat. I would see their entire countenance change after they were able to consume some food at church. Since we had obtained some vital statistics regarding the socio-economic conditions of our area therefore, we knew there was a need in the community to feed children. We could see the need for food as an issue every Sunday at our own church especially with the high unemployment rate of our members.

After receiving state approval to become a Sponsor of the SFSP, we began that first summer by placing a sign on the church lawn, advertising that free meals were available for children 9 a.m. to 1 p.m. We had a consistent number of children coming to the church everyday to receive free breakfast and free lunch meals Monday through Friday. We were also able to recruit and train five other sites, and we prepared and delivered meals to those sites as well. During that first summer, we prepared and delivered over 20,000 meals to children. At the time of such humble beginnings, especially with such a small congregation we never knew how God would use us to feed so many children in the Atlanta Metropolitan area.

As an Administrative Sponsor of SFSP, BOLD Ministries provides free summer meals to children eighteen years, and under at programs and organizations located in areas of need throughout the Atlanta Metropolitan Area. One of the most important criteria for the program is that all feeding sites must be located in an area where at least 50% or more of the children receive free or reduced meals during the school year. During the summer months, many children still need to receive nutritional meals in order to stay healthy and have a great start to the next school year.

Across the nation, approximately 22 million children receive free or reduced meals during the school year. During the summer months out of that same number, only 3 million children receive free meals. These statistics inform that the nation has a large gap in nutrition services to school age children. During the summer months, many children are hungry and their families have no way of making ends meet to feed their children. The SFSP is just one program that provides an option to meet the hunger needs of children in America.

In the capacity as an Administrative Sponsor, BOLD Ministries has the responsibility of organizing and convening several organizations in the local community as well as in outlying areas. The management of the SFSP has become a very wide scale project during the summer months and continues to increase exponentially each year because of the growing need for food for children. The SFSP project entails collaboration, outreach, training, and coordination of resources in order to operate as a successful project reaching hundreds of children each day with free meals.

Over the past ten years, the service that BOLD Ministries provides through the SFSP has progressively increased every year. We are currently serving over eight counties within the Atlanta Metropolitan area. This expansion of services allows us the opportunity to feed more children each year and meet their hunger needs. For instance, our statistics on the number of meals we provided, and the number of sites served are as follows:

- In 2009, 5 sites with 20,000 meals served
- In 2010, 15 sites with 49,000 meals served
- In 2011, 27 sites with 80,000 meals served
- In 2012, 53 sites with 149,000 meals served
- In 2013, 60 sites with over 160,000 meals served
- In 2014, 62 sites with 189,965 meals served
- In 2015, 65 sites with 170,778 meals served
- In 2016, 83 sites with 185,375 meals served
- In 2017, 65 sites with 202,012 meals served
- In 2018, 80 sites with 219,961 meals served

These statistics reflect meals provided to children at feeding sites just during the summer months. Again, these statistics are a key indication of the need for food for children in America, more specifically the Atlanta Metropolitan area in the state of Georgia.

In the summer of 2013, God put it on my heart to reach out to a different community than the summer programs that we typically serve. I knew of a low-income community that had a high population of Latinos living there that is a very impoverished area. Somehow, I wanted to figure out how we could reach that community. I began by looking for a Bilingual staff member to work for BOLD Ministries this particular summer. As God would have it, a woman from Cuba responded to the job announcement we placed with Department of Labor. Not only did she speak fluent Spanish, but she also expressed to me that God had placed the desire on her heart to minister to the Latino community. It was a match made in heaven.

One bright summer day as we headed for this densely populated community, we met some women from the community and my staff began to converse with them in Spanish. This was the beginning of a connection for BOLD Ministries in the community. We began to distribute fliers written in Spanish into the community, and within one week, we had 100 children signed up to receive free summer lunches. Before the summer was over, we were feeding 300 children a day in this community alone.

One of the biggest impacts for me of sponsoring the SFSP is the feedback I received from one of the Hispanic mothers. She expressed to us how happy she was that BOLD Ministries came to this community to provide free lunches and snacks. Many of the families in this community do not have jobs because of their skill sets, language barriers, and sometimes because of their status, so they face insurmountable odds in feeding their families. With the daily challenges the families face, they struggle to make ends meet through each month. Some examples follow that demonstrate some of the challenges faced by the children and families in the communities that we serve.

An 8-year old boy and his mother lost their sole provider due to some extenuating circumstances. When the summer food program started this young boy would not leave the house. I was told that he was so distraught about his family situation that, all he would do is cry. His mom knew the boy would greatly benefit from our program, so she started volunteering and would bring him with her to the community center. Slowly, the boy started engaging with the other children, eating lunch with them and even playing in the community center

In addition to serving as a Sponsor of the SFSP, in 2013, BOLD Ministries launched Project L.E.A.P., an afterschool program located in a community with at-risk children facing cultural and language barriers. Project L.E.A.P. is another avenue where BOLD Ministries can address hunger issues by providing free snack and supper meals to the children. BOLD Ministries continues to increase opportunities to serve children in need and help to promote the national campaign "No Kid Hungry."

Being a part of this summer food project, really gave me the opportunity to see that children needed food. In one county we serve there are over 11,000 children that are eligible to receive free or reduced school meals. This provides an indication of what the statistics are like in Georgia alone.

In a larger context, there are many families facing hunger not only in this county but also in the entire state, in America and in the world. This case study is just a small sampling of children and families facing hunger right here in Georgia, in America. This case study looks at addressing hunger locally, but by no means do I want to take for granted the 400 million children living in poverty around the world.[1] The question I ask, "What should be the Christian response to hunger?"

---

[1] "Progress on Poverty, But 1.2 Billion Still Live on the Extremes." *America* 209, no. 12: 8-9. *Religion and Philosophy Collection*, EBSCO*host* (accessed March 23, 2014).

INTRODUCTION

I have become very passionate about fighting hunger in America because of all the small, hungry faces I see not just during the summer, but also all year round. Across the nation, 22 million children, who typically receive free or reduced meals during the school year, suffer from hunger when school is out. For this very reason, through BOLD Ministries we are trying to make an impact in the fight against hunger, by feeding children 18 and under during the summer months and afterschool as well.

Hunger in America is real and still very apparent in the year 2019. While Christians are giving less and less into their communities there continues to be a growing need for food. "In a given week in the United States, an estimated 7 million people..." receive meals "at emergency feeding sites."[2] According to the 2013 Economic Research Service at the USDA, a report on food insecurity indicates that 49 million people in the United States (U.S.) are living in food insecure households and 15.9 million of that total are children.[3]

There are people living in the U.S. who have irregular eating

---

[2] George McGovern, Bob Doyle, Donald E. Messer, *Ending Hunger Now: A Challenge to Persons of Faith* (Minneapolis: Fortress Press, 2005), 2.
[3] Alisha Coleman-Jensen, William McFall, and Mark Nord, "Food Insecurity in Households with Children: Prevalence, Severity, and Household Characteristics 2010-11," *United States Department of Agriculture, Economic Research Service,* (May 2013), https://www.ers.usda.gov/topics/food-nutrition-assistance/food-security-in-the-us/ (accessed May 12, 2019).

patterns and who miss a meal at least one day or more per week. This irregularity initially called "hunger," but now the government wants to use a term that is less emotive so now they term this issue as "very low food security."[4] "Leaders of Bread for the World… point out that in America "one child in five lives in poverty" and "one child in five lives in a food-insecure household."[5]

The USDA report defines food insecurity as "Limited or uncertain availability of nutritionally adequate and safe foods or limited or uncertain ability to acquire acceptable foods in socially acceptable ways."[6] High food insecurity rates coupled with the rising costs of food increase the lack of food for children in the U.S. The following statistics from the Georgia State Food Bank are a major indication that validates the need for food for children in Georgia:

- Twenty percent of Georgians–nearly 1 in 5 Georgians are food insecure, which is well above the national average.
- Twenty-eight point eight percent of children in Georgia (1 in 4 children)–live in food insecure households. This means that more than 700,000 children in Georgia have been hungry without access to food in one of the wealthiest nations in the world.
- Thirty-nine percent of food insecure children in Georgia live in households above poverty and likely ineligible for any federal food nutrition programs. These are the children of working families. The term "working poor" is a reality in today's economy.

---

[4] David Beckmann, *Exodus from Hunger: We Are Called to Change the Politics of Hunger* (Louisville, KY: Westminster John Knox Press, 2010), 23.
[5] McGovern, "Ending Hunger Now," 6.
[6] "Food Security in the U.S.," *United States Department of Agriculture, Economic Research Service*, August 19, 2013. http://www.ers.usda.gov/topics/food-nutrition-assistance/food-security-in-the-us/measurement.aspx (March 22, 2014).

- Unemployment and underemployment are driving the increase in demand for food in Georgia.
- Seniors with special dietary needs and larger households due to the economic distress of family members are increasingly turning to food pantries for help.
- Hunger in Georgia is not limited to the homeless and unemployed. Working families are struggling as well.[7]

With the problem of food insecurity and the number of children that are hungry in America, several problems, and issues can arise. Some of the problems that food-insecurity can cause for children are:

- Food-insecure children are 90% more likely to have their overall health reported as "fair/poor" rather than "excellent/good" than kids from food-secure homes.
- Food insecurity is linked to increased hospitalizations, developmental problems, headaches, stomach aches, and even colds.
- When children eat breakfast, they tend to consume more nutrients and experience lower obesity rates.
- Hunger in childhood has been linked to significant health problems in adulthood.[8]

The focus of this book is concerning hunger in America, and what should be the Christian response. More specifically, there is a focus on children because they are our future so I demonstrate an urgent need for action. Fighting childhood hunger is also important because of:

---

[7] Georgia State Food Bank, "Surprising Facts About Hunger," "http://georgiafoodbankassociation.org/make-a-difference/surprising-facts-about-hunger-in-georgia/ (accessed March 23, 2014).

[8] "Food is fuel. Without it, a child can't live up to her full potential," *Share Our Strength*, 2013, http://www.nokidhungry.org/problem/nutrition-child-development (accessed March 23, 2014).

Cognition and Academic Affects

- Undernourished children 0-3 years of age cannot learn as much, as fast or as well.
- Lack of enough nutritious food impairs a child's ability to concentrate and perform well in school.
Emotional and Social Well-Being Affects
- Children who regularly do not get enough nutritious food to eat have significantly higher levels of behavioral, emotional, and academic problems and become more aggressive and anxious.
- Teens who regularly do not get enough to eat are more likely to be suspended from school and have difficulty getting along with other kids.[9]

I present this case study to stir, to move, and, to compel Christians to action in regards to ending hunger in the name of Jesus Christ. I lay out compelling reasons biblically, historically, and, theologically, why Christians should respond to the call to feed hungry children. I pray that this book liberates Christians, to take action for the children in our neighborhoods, in our state, in our country and in the world who need food.

---

[9] "Hunger Facts," *Share Our Strength*, http://nokidhungry2.org/hunger-facts (accessed March 16, 2014).

BIBLICAL RESPONSE TO THE POOR & TO HUNGER

Hunger is a human condition where people do not have enough food to eat. In the Greek language λιμός, means the desire for food.[10] The Greek word ʹebhyōn means "desirous," "needy," or "poor." With both Greek words speaking to desires and needs, throughout this book when I speak about the poor, I also speak concerning the desire and need for food, which spells out hunger. The Bible also describes hunger in several passages as famine.

When I speak of the poor I am also including children who usually fall into this category as a result of their family's economic situation or because they are orphans. From birth, children are dependent upon their family and/or caregivers to provide their basic needs including food. Oftentimes the family fails to make this provision for many different reasons. However, the Bible makes a compelling argument regarding how Christians are to respond to the call of hunger and to the poor. It is evident by these arguments that God is concerned for the poor.

Throughout the Bible are key scriptures that substantiate the claim that God cares about poor people, and the creator designed a

---

[10] The desire for food, a physiological sensation associated with emptiness of the stomach, and dependent on some state of the mucous membrane; (2) starvation as the effect of want of food. The International Standard Bible Encyclopedia.

system that would meet their needs. God provided laws to Moses that protected the poor. In Isa 58:6-7, the Bible clearly states that we are to share food with the hungry.[11] Isaiah 58:10-12 also demonstrates how God guided the Israelites to take care of the poor. The scripture provides a conditional statement that says if we offer our food to the hungry, then God will bless the people in many ways.[12]

God provided for the Israelites as they were in the wilderness as evidenced in Neh 9:15.[13] God is *"Jehovah Jireh,"* a provider as given by Abraham in Gen 22:14.[14] As Christians, God provides many examples of how we should pattern our lives. When the people were hungry, God fed them with manna and quail. They never had to want for anything as they followed God under the leadership of Moses.

In OT times, according to the law, reapers were to leave something in their fields and not reap from every corner, but they were to leave some parts of the field untouched. If the reapers drop some of the crops while harvesting their fields, they are to leave those droppings for the poor so that they can come and glean in the fields as well. Gleaning is the process of gathering grain or the harvest left

---

[11] All scripture citations are from the New Revised Standard Version unless otherwise noted. **Isaiah 58:6-7** Is not this the fast that I choose: to loose the bonds of injustice, to undo the thongs of the yoke, to let the oppressed go free, and to break every yoke?
Is it not to share your bread with the hungry, and bring the homeless poor into your house; when you see the naked, to cover them, and not to hide yourself from your own kin?

[12] Full text provided in Appendix A.

[13] **Nehemiah 9:15** For their hunger you gave them bread from heaven, and for their thirst you brought water for them out of the rock, and you told them to go in to possess the land that you swore to give them.

[14] **Genesis 22:14 (ASV)** And Abraham called the name of that place Jehovah-jireh. As it is said to this day, In the mount of Jehovah it shall be provided.

in a field by reapers.[15] Mosaic Law required leaving this portion so that the poor, widows, and, aliens might have a means of earning a living and surviving. This law found in Lev 19:9-10 provides a way for the people to feed and take care of the hungry.[16]

Additionally Deut 24:21 states, "When you gather the grapes of your vineyard, do not glean what is left; it shall be for the alien, the orphan, and the widow. This scripture reinforces the law found in Lev 19:9-10, which instructs the people to leave the corners of the field, which are the gleanings, for the poor. God reinforces the law by spelling it out clearly to the Israelites.

After leaving Egypt and wandering in the wilderness, God provided food for the children of Israel through various miracles. Exodus 16:2-18 demonstrates how God brought the provision to the Israelites.[17] After hearing, the cries of the children of Israel, and their murmurings God spoke to Moses and gave him clear instructions for the people to obtain the provision of food.

God provided bread from heaven, which the people called "Manna" and instructed the Israelites on how to gather the bread each day. On the sixth day, the people were to gather twice as much so they would have food for the seventh or Sabbath day without having to work. As if that was not enough, God even provided the Israelites with meat by causing quail to cover their campgrounds in the evening time. The Israelites were able to catch the quail with

---

[15] The process of gathering grain or produce left in a field by reapers or on a vine or tree by pickers. Mosaic law required leaving this portion so that the poor and aliens might have a means of earning a living. Holman Bible Dictionary.

[16] Leviticus 19:9-10 When you reap the harvest of your land, you shall not reap to the very edges of your field, or gather the gleanings of your harvest. [10] You shall not strip your vineyard bare, or gather the fallen grapes of your vineyard; you shall leave them for the poor and the alien: I am the LORD your God.

[17] Full text provided in Appendix B.

little or no effort. God provided bread and meat for the Israelites to take care of their hunger so that no one lacked.

Ruth 2 is an awesome example that demonstrates how the law of the land met a family's needs.[18] After returning home from Moab, Naomi and her daughter-in-law Ruth found themselves in need of food and in need of a way to survive. Naomi traveled back to Bethlehem after her husband and two sons died. There was famine in the land of Moab, so Naomi decided to return home to her people. As a means of survival, Naomi instructed Ruth concerning gleaning so that they two could survive the famine.

Biblical law found in Deut 23:24-25 allowed an individual to go into their neighbor's vineyard and eat, as many grapes until they were full, but the law did not allow them to carry any away in containers.[19] The law also allowed an individual to pluck corn from a neighbors' vineyard with their hands but they could not use any instruments to pluck. The poor could also glean from any forgotten sheaves left in the fields. Not only did the OT indicate how God provided for the poor and hungry, but the NT also reveals through Jesus Christ how to care for the poor.

Jesus is an awesome example of how we should treat the poor and he led by example. Beckmann points out that in the book of Luke "Jesus announces himself as the embodiment of God's messianic promises, including justice for people in need.[20] In Luke 4:18, Jesus says, "The Spirit of the Lord is upon me, because he has anointed me to bring good news to the poor." In Matt 15:32-38, Jesus again

---

[18] Full text provided in Appendix C.

[19] **Deuteronomy 23:24-25 (NRSV)** [24] If you go into your neighbor's vineyard, you may eat your fill of grapes, as many as you wish, but you shall not put any in a container. [25] If you go into your neighbor's standing grain, you may pluck the ears with your hand, but you shall not put a sickle to your neighbor's standing grain.

[20] Beckmann, "Exodus from Hunger," 71.

reveals his compassion on the poor by feeding the multitude that was hungry.[21]

In Matt 25:34-40, Jesus speaks again concerning the poor and hungry.[22] Jesus demonstrates in this passage of scripture that when people bless the poor they in essence bless him. When we bless others who are less fortunate than ourselves, than we bless our Lord and Savior at the same time. This is a clear indication of how Jesus wants us to treat the poor and the needy.

After Pentecost, the early Christians were on one accord, so much so that people brought their belongings and laid them at the feet of the Apostles. As noted in Acts 4:32-35 there was no lack, because the Apostles sold all things and distributed the goods to meet the needs of the people.[23] In Matt 26:11, Jesus says, "For you always have the poor with you, but you will not always have me." I believe that Jesus made this statement to let Christians know that the poor will always be among us and it is our responsibility to meet their needs.

Mark 10:21 provides an example of how we can meet the needs of the poor by selling what we have and giving to the poor.[24] In James 2, the Bible instructs us that if someone is in need then we should try to meet that need and not just send him or her away. The Bible gives us numerous examples of how we are to treat those in

---

[21] Full text provided in Appendix D.

[22] Full text provided in Appendix E.

[23] **Acts 4:32-35 (NRSV)** [32] Now the whole group of those who believed were of one heart and soul, and no one claimed private ownership of any possessions, but everything they owned was held in common. [33] With great power the apostles gave their testimony to the resurrection of the Lord Jesus, and great grace was upon them all. [34] There was not a needy person among them, for as many as owned lands or houses sold them and brought the proceeds of what was sold. [35] They laid it at the apostles' feet, and it was distributed to each as any had need.

[24] **Mark 10:21 (NRSV)** Jesus, looking at him, loved him and said, "You lack one thing; go, sell what you own, and give the money to the poor, and you will have treasure in heaven; then come, follow me."

need. We have clear instructions concerning sharing and caring for our neighbor with food.

In Luke 16:19-25 we find the parable of Lazarus and the rich man.[25] Lazarus was poor and hungry during his life on earth. He sat by the table of the rich man to try and even catch crumbs from the food that the rich man ate. From the Bible text, it is evident that Lazarus suffered hunger on many occasions. The passage of scripture does not indicate that the rich man ever offered Lazarus a morsel of food to eat. Even though Lazarus suffered poverty on earth, he found favor with God in the βασιλεία kingdom of God. Then we see the tables turned and Lazarus was in the bosom of Abraham, while the rich man suffered in Hades. It is better to share and give to the poor while here on earth and our reward will be greater in heaven.

---

[25] Full text provided in Appendix F.

HISTORICAL VIEW
OF POVERTY

St. Francis of Assisi really stands out as a dominant figure in church history whose life really speaks to hunger and poverty. Groomed to take over his father's business St. Francis turned his back on the family business and wealth to begin a journey down a different path. Growing up he was fairly well off, since his parent's commercial ventures granted St Francis money, which he lavished on food and drinks. St. Francis was a proud and flamboyant young man and on several occasions, flaunted his wealth.

Even as a young man St. Francis had compassion for the poor and he did have instances of generosity. He began by preparing meals at home to give to the poor. He became involved in feudal wars and was captured and imprisoned at one point in his life. It was during this time that St. Francis contemplated what he would do with his life.

St. Francis began having feelings of strong detachment from material possessions. He believed that God was calling him to preach and teach the Gospels so he began pointing his life in that direction. Following the examples of Jesus Christ living and interacting with the poor, St. Francis pledged himself to what he termed as "Lady Poverty."[26] From that point forward, St. Francis began to give to

---

[26] Michael Robson, *St. Francis of Assisi: The Legend and the Life*, (New York: Wellington House, 1997), 94.

people in need whenever they crossed his path. On one occasion, he gave up his own clothes to meet the needs of another man. St. Francis believed that his sacrifice and care for the poor was the road to "perfect discipleship."

Monasticism was growing rapidly during medieval times, which greatly influenced St. Francis. He began spending more and more time at various monasteries. St. Francis began aligning his life to that of the disciples where he believed the message of Jesus Christ pointed him to a life of poverty. He believed it was a personal calling from God to live a life of penance.

St. Francis begins a new fraternity at a church called "The Portiuncula." He wrote a "Rule of 1221" for the fraternity, specifying a requirement that the friars live in obedience "without anything of their own and to walk in the footsteps of Jesus Christ."[27] Along with this requirement, St. Francis presented a way of life known as "voluntary poverty" where the men renounced material possessions. This period marked the beginning of the Franciscan order and others came to join the new fraternity as well.

St. Francis modeled the Christian response to poverty and hunger by living his life void of materialism. He was an awesome example for his followers as he followed the steps of Jesus Christ.

Clare a lifelong friend of St. Francis also converted and embraced a life of "evangelical poverty, contemplation, and, asceticism."[28] Clare had a strong compassion for the poor as well even though she was born into a wealthy family. Innocent IV confirmed a new Rule written by Clare, which was notably a first for women living during the Middle Ages. As a follower of St. Francis, Clare begins a new order, known as the "Poor Clares."[29] This new order also embraced

---

[27] Ibid. 110.

[28] Ibid. 187.

[29] Joanne Schatzlein, "Francis of Assisi 1181-1220: Christian History Timeline," *Christian History* Issue 42 (1994), under "ChristianHistory.net," http://www.christianitytoday.com/ch/1994/issue42/4226.html (accessed May 12, 2019).

poverty and continued the work of St. Francis of Assisi to support the poor.

The Donatist movement also provided support for the poor and sick with income from properties that they accumulated. The Donatists also seen as an "African continental religious movement" also practiced personal poverty, which was included in the mendicant orders.[30] They believed that all Christians should practice sharing with those in need while practicing virtues of poverty, love, and, simplicity. The reason for the establishment of these movements along with others was to challenge the existing Roman religious structures.

Monasticism originated in the second half of the 3rd century as a protest movement against conditions of life in the Roman Empire.[31] People began detaching themselves from the life of society and others began to follow suit. Early Western Monasticism responded to the concerns of Christians in quest of justice and a holy alliance. As old monastic orders more influenced by political structures and their own wealth grew dim, new monastic orders began emerging.

One movement in particular is the "Apostolic Poverty Movement" which was generally a revolutionary reform movement."[32] The basic tenets of this movement are:

> They were all directed against the political and economic identification of the church with brutal and corrupt power structures, and against the worldly luxury of the hierarchy. They demanded an immediate return to the apostolic simplicity, poverty, and humility of the first Christians. While these demands were absolute and immediate

---

[30] Vatro Murvar. 1975. "Toward a sociological theory of religious movements." *Journal For The Scientific Study Of Religion* 14, no. 3: 229-256. *ATLA Religion Database with ATLASerials*, EBSCO*host* (accessed March 18, 2014).

[31] Ibid. 240.

[32] Ibid. 242.

in relation to the clergy and hierarchy, the hope was frequently expressed that through the clergy's example the society at large eventually would be induced to practice Christian ethics by accepting voluntary poverty and simplicity. The urgency was dramatized by the presence of masses of desperately poor people, orphans, and the aged who ought to be fed and clothed if Christianity was to make any sense.[33]

The founders of this movement were mostly monks, priests and other people of lower social classes. In essence, this movement sought social and economic justice for the poor but seemed to neglect their religious purposes.

Another view from the 4th century church include that of three Greek bishops known as the Great Cappadocians which include Basil of Caesarea, his brother Gregory of Nyssa and their friend Gregory of Nazianzus.[34] They brought to the forefront issues on poverty and wealth and viewed the fair and loving treatment of the poor as crucial to Christian conduct and more importantly to salvation. The three bishops had a concern of drawing the attention of their social group to the situations and needs of the poor.

The bishops wanted to get the attention of their wealthy congregants to share what they had with the poor and the beggars in the town square. Even though these young men came from Christian families socially connected in their communities, they had a concern for those less fortunate. All three bishops composed sermons on love of and service to the poor.[35]

After a drought during the summer of 369, that left Anatolia with a shortage of food and water, Basil preached three powerful

---

[33] Ibid. 242.

[34] Daniel G. Groody, ed., *The Option for the Poor in Christian Theology* (Notre Dame: University of Notre Dame Press, 2007), 78.

[35] Ibid. 80.

sermons in an effort to convince the wealthier members of the congregation to share their food supplies with those who were in need. Basil urged the congregants to act on this sharing as part of their Christian obligation. Basil's sermon:

> Jesus's portrait of the "rich fool" in Luke 12:16-21 subtitled "On Greed," It argues that all the earth's produce is given to us by God for common use and that individuals are simply stewards of a common supply.[36]

Basil believed if people had a surplus, then they needed to share it with those in need. Basil practiced what he preached by personally working in a soup kitchen during the famine and building a hospice for those who were sick.

Basil's brother Gregory of Nyssa also preached powerful sermons on serving and helping the poor. As part of a Lenten sequence, Gregory preached concerning self-restraint and self-control during the season of Lent with concern for the poor in their city. He asked his congregation to also share and give to the poor. Gregory states, "the poor whom we have helped will be our advocates before, God" bearing the face of Christ.[37]

Basil's friend Gregory of Nazianzus also chimed in with his sermon, "On Loving the Poor."[38] Gregory of Nazianzus believed that love for your fellow man and woman expressed through love of the poor is one of the greatest virtues of a Christian. He spoke of the lepers that were roaming the streets because of rejection by friends and family and were in need of food and shelter. Those who are sick sometimes become poor because of circumstances beyond their control.

The three bishops of Cappadocia preached to their congregations

---

[36] Ibid.

[37] Ibid. 82.

[38] Ibid.

in hopes of moving them to action for the poor and marginalized. Their message was to Christians as to how they should live their lives and how they should treat the poor. Again, the theme of God's concern for the poor is evident even in this early church tradition.

THEOLOGICAL VIEW ON POVERTY

Gustavo Gutiérrez, a theologian who contributed to biblical theology with terms from liberation theology such as *"the poor, liberation, and option for the poor."*[39] Gutiérrez at the heart of the liberation theological movement conveyed the importance of justice and liberation for the poor and the oppressed. Liberation theology is a wakeup call for many Christians, calling for action in the fight for the poor against hunger and oppression.

Our Creator is a God of justice who has compassion for the poor, oppressed, and, marginalized. Psalm 146:7-9 reveals that God provides food for the poor, justice for the oppressed, and, takes care of the widows and the orphans.[40] God is a liberator who intervenes for the people.

According to Gustavo Gutiérrez, Christ as a liberator for the poor and impoverished chose to live with the poor.[41] Gutiérrez also says, "The Bible speaks of liberation and justice as opposed to

---

[39] Ibid. 41.

[40] **Psalm 146:7-9 (NRSV)** who executes justice for the oppressed; who gives food to the hungry. The LORD sets the prisoners free; the LORD opens the eyes of the blind. The LORD lifts up those who are bowed down; the LORD loves the righteous. The LORD watches over the strangers; he upholds the orphan and the widow, but the way of the wicked he brings to ruin.

[41] Gustavo Gutierrez, *The Power of the Poor in History* (Maryknoll, NY: Orbis Books, 1983), 13.

slavery and the humiliation of the poor."[42] Biblical theology looks at poverty as an important theme in the Bible naturally connected to the framework of oppression. People still say that people are poor or hungry because they are lazy or they simply do not care. Liberation theology changed this narrow way of thinking when reading the Bible in a Latin American context.

Children all over the world are suffering because of hunger. The children do not suffer because they committed a sin nor do they suffer because their parents are lazy. Many children are suffering due to an unequal distribution across the world of food and wealth. The poor are not outcast of society, but instead they are part of God's special society, that receives unconditional love.

Gutiérrez presents "an option for the poor" consisting of grace, love and mercy which is demonstrated through the life of Jesus Christ.[43] God reveals an option for the poor through Jesus' birth in a lowly manger. Jesus was born into poverty, lived in poverty and died in poverty. With the living example of Jesus Christ, God's beloved son, we know that God cares for the poor and that poverty is not a result of sin.

God demonstrates this option of solidarity with the poor when we look at the social location of Jesus. Overall, in the Bible, we see God as creator and liberator of the poor, oppressed, and, marginalized. God's option for the poor is not just a biblical theme but it is a theological framework for Christians to follow.

Gustavo Gutiérrez also presents another theological perspective on, "God and the Poor" by looking at Job's life.[44] In his perception of Job's monologue, Gutiérrez says that innocence is not simply individual uprightness, but rather an individual's treatment of the poor. Gutiérrez stresses that the poor are the beloved of God, and includes Job's thoughts on the matter:

---

[42] Ibid. 18.

[43] Groody, "The Option for the Poor," 45.

[44] Gustavo Gutiérrez, *On Job: God-Talk and the Suffering of the Innocent*, ((Maryknoll, NY: Orbis Books, 1986), 39.

Job 29:12-17

¹² because I delivered the poor who cried, and the orphan who had no helper.

¹³ The blessing of the wretched came upon me, and I caused the widow's heart to sing for joy.

¹⁴ I put on righteousness, and it clothed me; my justice was like a robe and a turban.

¹⁵ I was eyes to the blind, and feet to the lame.

¹⁶ I was a father to the needy, and I championed the cause of the stranger.

¹⁷ I broke the fangs of the unrighteous, and made them drop their prey from their teeth.

Job reminisces on happier times and tries to convey that he was a just and an upright man, helping the poor, the orphan, and, the stranger.

Gutiérrez expresses that uprightness or justice (δίκη) and judgment (αἴσθησις) as key words in the Bible. Practicing justice and judgment is to follow God's commandment. Job makes the practice of these commandments, as a central part of his life. Gutiérrez says, "uprightness and judgment cannot be promoted in the abstract but only in relation to the inhuman situation in which orphans, widows, and, strangers live ("orphans, widows, and strangers" is a classical biblical synonym for "the poor").[45]

We see that Job calls God "the Father of the poor," so Gutiérrez ties this to how Christians are to treat the poor as though they are family and not strangers.[46] In this context, he uses the word "Father" to represent determination as well as an affectionate relationship. God does not punish the poor but instead cares for them as friends. When we give to the poor, we are in essence giving unto God.

---

[45] Ibid. 40.

[46] **Job 29:16 (NRSV)** ¹⁶ I was a father to the needy, and I championed the cause of the stranger.

Proverbs 19:17 says that whoever is kind to the poor lends to the Lord.

Job was a generous man as displayed by his acts of mercy as expressed in Job 29. Job provides detail of how he has helped the poor: by providing food for the hungry, helping the orphans, providing clothing and shelter for those in need, and, justice for those who are innocent. Gutiérrez expresses so eloquently that the "defense of the poor requires their liberation and resistance to those who oppress and exploit them."[47]

Today, there exists a major spokesperson that has that same liberating passion for the poor, and that is Pope Francis. Several speeches by Pope Francis convey a message of genuine concern and care for the poor. An article in the Huffington Post describes the Pope in this context:

> Pope Francis is making his mark as one Catholic Church's more humble Popes by eschewing luxurious vestments in favor of simple white robes, as well as staying in modest housing instead of the Papal apartments, and using a Ford Focus instead of the Benz.
>
> He has also made a number of decisive statements about the importance of humility, urging solidarity with the poor and needy, and chose the name "Francis" to evoke St. Francis of Assisi, who stands for peace, austerity, and poverty.

---

[47] Gutiérrez, "On Job," 40.

In an early speech at Vatican City after his elevation to Pope, he commented, "Oh, how I would like a poor Church, and for the poor."[48]

An International Bulletin reports Pope Francis as a man of radiant simplicity and genuine humility, a man of intellect and of compassion.[49] The Pope has taken measures to consider the poor and to involve the Catholic Church in the issue of hunger. He expresses the love of God by his love of the people, and his compassion for those who are suffering.

The words of Pope Francis during his public addresses have signaled a shift of emphasis toward social justice.[50] His concern for the poor and oppressed models the behavior that all Christians should have toward those in need. The writer expresses the significant call of Pope Francis, which is to have "a poor church for the poor."[51] He has already made himself an example to the world by reflecting a humble spirit and by refusing the excessive accessories typically worn by the papacy.

Liberation Theology speaks to an urgent need for Christians to respond and "involve themselves in the work of liberating" the oppressed and for Christians to establish a solidarity with the poor and oppressed.[52] Worship is not authentic without the love for God and the poor and oppressed.

In the words of theologian Dietrich Bonhoeffer, "The test of the

---

[48] Yasmine Hafiz, "Pope Francis Quotes On The Poor" *The Huffington Post*, U.S. edition, August 19, 2013. http://www.huffingtonpost.com/2013/08/19/pope-francis-quotes-poor_n_3780816.html (accessed May 12, 2019).

[49] Theodora Bilocura "Pope Francis, Christian Mission, and the Church of Saint Francis." *International Bulletin Of Missionary Research* 37, no. 3: 165-166. *Religion and Philosophy Collection*, EBSCO*host* (accessed March 24, 2014)

[50] Ibid.

[51] Ibid.

[52] Gutierrez, "Power of the Poor," 29.

morality of a society is how it treats its children."[53] McGovern also points out another Bonhoeffer quote,

> "To allow the hungry man to remain hungry would be blasphemy against God and one's neighbor, for what is nearest to God is precisely the need of one's neighbor."[54]

Bonhoeffer, well known for his writings on justice and ethics, describes the way God desires for Christians to respond to people who are suffering. One of the main points he stresses is that sharing is key to a spiritual walk with God. "Bonhoeffer wrote:

It is for the love of Christ, which belongs as much to the hungry man as to myself, that I share my bread with him and that I share my dwelling with the homeless. If the hungry man does not attain to faith, then the fault falls on those who refused him bread. To provide the hungry man with bread is to prepare the way for the coming of grace."[55]

---

[53] McGovern, "Ending Hunger Now," 6.
[54] Ibid. 12.
[55] Ibid.

PASTORAL RESPONSE TO HUNGER

As Christians, we should focus more on community issues and not just on internal issues at our individual churches, when our hearts are in the right place. Deuteronomy 15:11 states, "Since there will never cease to be some in need on the earth, I therefore command you, "Open your hand to the poor and needy neighbor in your land." This scripture provides clarity regarding how believers in God are to treat the poor.

Proverbs 22:9 also provides instruction where the text directs believers to share your food with the poor.[56] Proverbs 28:27 speaks a blessing into the life of the believer who gives to the poor.[57] Matthew 6:2 instructs Christians how to give to charity or to people in need without broadcasting when we give.[58]

The English word "alms" is an abridged form of the Greek

---

[56] Proverbs 22:9 Those who are generous are blessed, for they share their bread with the poor.

[57] Proverbs 28:27 Whoever gives to the poor will lack nothing, but one who turns a blind eye will get many a curse.

[58] **Matthew 6:2-4** 2 "So whenever you give alms, do not sound a trumpet before you, as the hypocrites do in the synagogues and in the streets, so that they may be praised by others. Truly I tell you, they have received their reward. 3 But when you give alms, do not let your left hand know what your right hand is doing, 4 so that your alms may be done in secret; and your Father who sees in secret will reward you.

word, ἐλεημοσύνη. As indicated in the Bible, almsgiving is a form of charity which we can still see evident today. Through almsgiving or charity is a way that Christians can continue in the faith and support the poor. Almsgiving also includes acts of kindness and justice as evidenced by two Greek words *Dikaiosúnē* and *eleēmosúnē.* As Christians, we are to promote charity not just by financial support of the poor but by the way, we act and treat the poor.

In Isa 58:6-7 the Bible states, "Deal thy bread to the hungry." When we share, we are helping and carrying out the work of the kingdom of God. When we fast, we can abstain from food for a day and the food that we do not eat we can give to the poor, the hungry, a food bank, or a family in need. God provides so many ways that we can minister and help others.

Proverbs 31:9-10 says to defend the rights of the poor and needy. We are to open our arms to the poor and extend our hands. In other words, we are to give to those in need. Luke 6:38 says to give and it shall be given unto you, good measure, pressed down and shaken together and running over.

There are numerous examples of giving to the poor in the Bible. If we want to use the Bible as a tool for our lives, then we can clearly see how God wants us to treat the poor. Nehemiah gave to the poor, Dorcas gave to the poor, Cornelius, Zaccheus, Job, Boaz, and, the Jerusalem church gave to the poor. The Bible presents clear written instructions for us to follow in discovering a Christian response in treatment of the poor. We are to give, share, and, help the poor and needy.

Christians can rediscover a biblical approach to life, if we just look for the golden nuggets available for us in the Bible. We should not become complacent and accept the status quo, but instead we have the opportunity to challenge the inequalities of power and fight for social justice. Most of all if we put on compassion like Jesus, it will bother us when we see a hungry child on television and not just ignore what we see and we will be aware of what is happening in our own country. I am all for global missions and trying to feed the world, but I believe that charity begins at home.

When you pray the Lord's Prayer and you say "Give us this day our daily bread" do we pray for those less fortunate than ourselves. We are not going to change the world unless we get our prayers right.[59] We need to make sure that our prayers include the poor, the hungry, and, the needy. When we participate in communion, we should keep in mind that Jesus shared the bread and the cup that we might also share with others. We should keep our prayers before God concerning not just our needs, but the needs of others as well. As Christians, we should pray for direction from God as to how we can serve, not just in our churches but in our communities as well.

Walk with God in an effort to bring about change. Build a strong relationship with God that will help lead us to the place that God wants us to be. Let the movement to fight hunger begin with God. Let God guide and direct us in how we should flow.

Be like Jesus in feeding the crowds, feeding the hungry and taking care of the poor. How can we expect the children to hear the good news of Jesus if they are hungry? Before Jesus spoke to the five thousand, he fed them first. Being more like Jesus entails serving the community before we began to evangelize.

In the fight against hunger, there exists a need for people in various avenues or disciplines in order to bring about change. Becoming a hunger advocate, is always a great place to start getting involved. Since the government continues to cut back on SNAP programs and other funding for nutrition programs, you can make your voice heard through your local senator or other grassroots efforts. Fight for political change, justice, and, equality for all people as a call to liberate the oppressed and marginalized.

In an effort to provide, some practical ways that you can get involved, I have listed several things you can do and various organizations that you can contact that are already involved in the

---

[59] Beckman, "Exodus from Hunger," 168.

fight for hunger. Some of the sites are feeding people in general, but since my focus is on children, I have included the organizations that are working with children first.[60] You can also fight hunger by providing information through literature, brochures, bulletin announcements, and, other various ways to promote interest and action for communities of faith to fight hunger.

- Movements: No Kid Hungry national campaign
- Start a Summer Food Site at your church or in your neighborhood
- Start a backpack program to provide food for children on the weekends.
- Volunteer at the local food bank
- Partner with Bread for the World
- Partner with CBF
- #EndHunger – Twitter
- Pray
- Become an Activist
- Contribute money to organizations already serving
- Engage your church
- Start a food bank
- Start a Soup Kitchen

The bottom line for Christians is to get involved. Hunger stops when we take a stand and take action. Let us not take a backseat to justice, but let us be in the forefront of seeking justice for the poor, the widow, and, the orphan. Let America hear your voice! Let the government hear your voice and speak for the children who cannot speak for themselves. McGovern speaks,

> "Being a Christian in the twenty-first century means not just testifying to the divine trinity, or

---

[60] See Appendix G for listings of websites serving children.

articulating a particular Christology, or declaring oneself "born again" or "liberal" or whatever. Rather, as the highest priority of faith and ethics, it includes thinking, praying, and acting to end human hunger and misery."[61]

---

[61] McGovern, "Ending Hunger Now," 99.

CONCLUSION

If we would just look around us, we can see that hunger is everywhere. Hunger has no color, no ethnicity, or race but it affects people from all walks of life. After seeing hungry children and I know that they are right here in my own backyard, I just feel so passionate about helping to feed. In the summertime, we go into neighborhoods where the children look with anticipation for the van or driver to pull into their complex delivering lunches.

If we see and we know that children right here in the Atlanta Metropolitan area are hungry, then why as Christians do we ignore the problem. The Bible provides an overwhelming response to what our response should be as Christians. I am so honored to serve hungry children summer after summer as long as God allows. Even with our efforts, there still exists, a large gap in the number of children that need food. Many children need the provision of free meals all year long.

If everyone participated in the fight for hunger and did their part, no child would go hungry in this country or even in the world. Most Americans spend frivolously and waste food every week that they do not eat, which can be available to children that are hungry. I hope and pray that we can make a difference in this generation, in this time and season, to help others who need support throughout our state and our nation. I pray that the readers can hear a compelling voice to feed God's children so that no kid is hungry in America!

APPENDIX A

Isaiah 58:6-7, 10-12

[10] if you offer your food to the hungry
and satisfy the needs of the afflicted,
then your light shall rise in the darkness
and your gloom be like the noonday.
[11] The LORD will guide you continually,
and satisfy your needs in parched places,
and make your bones strong;
and you shall be like a watered garden,
like a spring of water,
whose waters never fail.
[12] Your ancient ruins shall be rebuilt;
you shall raise up the foundations of many generations;
you shall be called the repairer of the breach,
the restorer of streets to live in.

APPENDIX B

Exodus 16:2-18

2 The whole congregation of the Israelites complained against Moses and Aaron in the wilderness.

3 The Israelites said to them, "If only we had died by the hand of the LORD in the land of Egypt, when we sat by the fleshpots and ate our fill of bread; for you have brought us out into this wilderness to kill this whole assembly with hunger."

4 Then the LORD said to Moses, "I am going to rain bread from heaven for you, and each day the people shall go out and gather enough for that day. In that way I will test them, whether they will follow my instruction or not.

5 On the sixth day, when they prepare what they bring in, it will be twice as much as they gather on other days."

6 So Moses and Aaron said to all the Israelites, "In the evening you shall know that it was the LORD who brought you out of the land of Egypt,

7 and in the morning you shall see the glory of the LORD, because he has heard your complaining against the LORD. For what are we, that you complain against us?"

8 And Moses said, "When the LORD gives you meat to eat in the evening and your fill of bread in the morning, because the LORD has heard the complaining that you utter against him—what are we? Your complaining is not against us but against the LORD."

⁹ Then Moses said to Aaron, "Say to the whole congregation of the Israelites, 'Draw near to the LORD, for he has heard your complaining.'"

¹⁰ And as Aaron spoke to the whole congregation of the Israelites, they looked toward the wilderness, and the glory of the LORD appeared in the cloud.

¹¹ The LORD spoke to Moses and said,

¹² "I have heard the complaining of the Israelites; say to them, 'At twilight you shall eat meat, and in the morning you shall have your fill of bread; then you shall know that I am the LORD your God.'"

¹³ In the evening quails came up and covered the camp; and in the morning there was a layer of dew around the camp.

¹⁴ When the layer of dew lifted, there on the surface of the wilderness was a fine flaky substance, as fine as frost on the ground.

¹⁵ When the Israelites saw it, they said to one another, "What is it?" For they did not know what it was. Moses said to them, "It is the bread that the LORD has given you to eat.

¹⁶ This is what the LORD has commanded: 'Gather as much of it as each of you needs, an omer to a person according to the number of persons, all providing for those in their own tents.'"

¹⁷ The Israelites did so, some gathering more, some less.

¹⁸ But when they measured it with an omer, those who gathered much had nothing over, and those who gathered little had no shortage; they gathered as much as each of them needed.

APPENDIX C

Ruth 2:1-23

[1] Now Naomi had a kinsman on her husband's side, a prominent rich man, of the family of Elimelech, whose name was Boaz.

[2] And Ruth the Moabite said to Naomi, "Let me go to the field and glean among the ears of grain, behind someone in whose sight I may find favor." She said to her, "Go, my daughter."

[3] So she went. She came and gleaned in the field behind the reapers. As it happened, she came to the part of the field belonging to Boaz, who was of the family of Elimelech.

[4] Just then Boaz came from Bethlehem. He said to the reapers, "The LORD be with you." They answered, "The LORD bless you."

[5] Then Boaz said to his servant who was in charge of the reapers, "To whom does this young woman belong?"

[6] The servant who was in charge of the reapers answered, "She is the Moabite who came back with Naomi from the country of Moab.

[7] She said, 'Please, let me glean and gather among the sheaves behind the reapers.' So she came, and she has been on her feet from early this morning until now, without resting even for a moment."

[8] Then Boaz said to Ruth, "Now listen, my daughter, do not go to glean in another field or leave this one, but keep close to my young women.

[9] Keep your eyes on the field that is being reaped, and follow behind them. I have ordered the young men not to bother you. If you get

thirsty, go to the vessels and drink from what the young men have drawn."

¹⁰ Then she fell prostrate, with her face to the ground, and said to him, "Why have I found favor in your sight, that you should take notice of me, when I am a foreigner?"

¹¹ But Boaz answered her, "All that you have done for your mother-in-law since the death of your husband has been fully told me, and how you left your father and mother and your native land and came to a people that you did not know before.

¹² May the LORD reward you for your deeds, and may you have a full reward from the LORD, the God of Israel, under whose wings you have come for refuge!"

¹³ Then she said, "May I continue to find favor in your sight, my lord, for you have comforted me and spoken kindly to your servant, even though I am not one of your servants."

¹⁴ At mealtime Boaz said to her, "Come here, and eat some of this bread, and dip your morsel in the sour wine." So she sat beside the reapers, and he heaped up for her some parched grain. She ate until she was satisfied, and she had some left over.

¹⁵ When she got up to glean, Boaz instructed his young men, "Let her glean even among the standing sheaves, and do not reproach her. ¹⁶ You must also pull out some handfuls for her from the bundles, and leave them for her to glean, and do not rebuke her."

¹⁷ So she gleaned in the field until evening. Then she beat out what she had gleaned, and it was about an ephah of barley.

¹⁸ She picked it up and came into the town, and her mother-in-law saw how much she had gleaned. Then she took out and gave her what was left over after she herself had been satisfied.

¹⁹ Her mother-in-law said to her, "Where did you glean today? And where have you worked? Blessed be the man who took notice of you." So she told her mother-in-law with whom she had worked, and said, "The name of the man with whom I worked today is Boaz."

²⁰ Then Naomi said to her daughter-in-law, "Blessed be he by the LORD, whose kindness has not forsaken the living or the dead!"

Naomi also said to her, "The man is a relative of ours, one of our nearest kin."

²¹ Then Ruth the Moabite said, "He even said to me, 'Stay close by my servants, until they have finished all my harvest.'"

²² Naomi said to Ruth, her daughter-in-law, "It is better, my daughter, that you go out with his young women, otherwise you might be bothered in another field."

²³ So she stayed close to the young women of Boaz, gleaning until the end of the barley and wheat harvests; and she lived with her mother-in-law.

APPENDIX D

Matthew 15:32-38

[32] Then Jesus called his disciples to him and said, "I have compassion for the crowd, because they have been with me now for three days and have nothing to eat; and I do not want to send them away hungry, for they might faint on the way."

[33] The disciples said to him, "Where are we to get enough bread in the desert to feed so great a crowd?"

[34] Jesus asked them, "How many loaves have you?" They said, "Seven, and a few small fish."

[35] Then ordering the crowd to sit down on the ground, .

[36] he took the seven loaves and the fish; and after giving thanks he broke them and gave them to the disciples, and the disciples gave them to the crowds.

[37] And all of them ate and were filled; and they took up the broken pieces left over, seven baskets full.

[38] Those who had eaten were four thousand men, besides women and children.

APPENDIX E

Matthew 25:34-40

34 Then the king will say to those at his right hand, 'Come, you that are blessed by my Father, inherit the kingdom prepared for you from the foundation of the world;

35 for I was hungry and you gave me food, I was thirsty and you gave me something to drink, I was a stranger and you welcomed me,

36 I was naked and you gave me clothing, I was sick and you took care of me, I was in prison and you visited me.'

37 Then the righteous will answer him, 'Lord, when was it that we saw you hungry and gave you food, or thirsty and gave you something to drink?

38 And when was it that we saw you a stranger and welcomed you, or naked and gave you clothing?

39 And when was it that we saw you sick or in prison and visited you?'

40 And the king will answer them, 'Truly I tell you, just as you did it to one of the least of these who are members of my family, you did it to me.'

APPENDIX F

Luke 16:19-25

[19] "There was a rich man who was dressed in purple and fine linen and who feasted sumptuously every day.

[20] And at his gate lay a poor man named Lazarus, covered with sores,

[21] who longed to satisfy his hunger with what fell from the rich man's table; even the dogs would come and lick his sores.

[22] The poor man died and was carried away by the angels to be with Abraham. The rich man also died and was buried.

[23] In Hades, where he was being tormented, he looked up and saw Abraham far away with Lazarus by his side.

[24] He called out, 'Father Abraham, have mercy on me, and send Lazarus to dip the tip of his finger in water and cool my tongue; for I am in agony in these flames.'

[25] But Abraham said, 'Child, remember that during your lifetime you received your good things, and Lazarus in like manner evil things; but now he is comforted here, and you are in agony.

APPENDIX G

Websites:

http://www.boldministries.org
http://georgiafoodbankassociation.org/
http://www.decal.ga.gov/Nutrition/NutritionServicesMain.aspx
www.nokidhungry.org
www.stophungernow.org
http://www.bread.org/
http://www.helpendhunger.org/
http://www.savethechildren.org
http://www.feedthechildren.org
http://www.childhungerendshere.com/index.html
http://www.ers.usda.gov/topics/food-nutrition-assistance/food-security-in-the-us/key-statistics-graphics.aspx
http://feedingamerica.org/SiteFiles/child-economy-study.pdf

BIBLIOGRAPHY

Beckmann, David. *Exodus from Hunger: We Are Called to Change the Politics of Hunger.* Louisville, KY: Westminster John Knox Press, 2010.

Bilocura, Theodora. "Pope Francis, Christian Mission, and the Church of Saint Francis." *International Bulletin Of Missionary Research* 37, no. 3: 165-166. *Religion and Philosophy Collection,* EBSCO*host* (accessed March 24, 2014)

Coleman-Jensen, Alisha, William McFall, and Mark Nord, "Food Insecurity in Households with Children: Prevalence, Severity, and Household Characteristics 2010-11," *United States Department of Agriculture, Economic Research Service,* (May 2013), http://www.ers.usda.gov/publications/eib-economic-information-bulletin/eib113.aspx (accessed March 22, 2014).

"Food Security in the U.S., " *United States Department of Agriculture, Economic Research Service,* August 19, 2013. http://www.ers.usda.gov/topics/food-nutrition-assistance/food-security-in-the-us/measurement.aspx (March 22, 2014).

"Food is fuel. Without it, a child can't live up to her full potential," *Share Our Strength,* 2013. http://www.nokidhungry.org/problem/nutrition-child-development (accessed March 23, 2014).

Ford, John T. 2010. "Handbook of U.S. theologies of liberation." *Religious Studies Review* 36, no. 2: 131-132. *ATLA Religion Database with ATLASerials*, EBSCO*host* (accessed January 27, 2014).

Georgia State Food Bank, "Surprising Facts About Hunger," "http://georgiafoodbankassociation.org/make-a-difference/surprising-facts-about-hunger-in-georgia/ (accessed March 23, 2014).

Groody, Daniel G. ed., *The Option for the Poor in Christian Theology.* Notre Dame: University of Notre Dame Press, 2007.

Gutiérrez, Gustavo. *The Power of the Poor in History.* Maryknoll, NY: Orbis Books, 1983.

Gutiérrez, Gustavo. *On Job: God-Talk and the Suffering of the Innocent.* Maryknoll, NY: Orbis Books, 1986.

Hafiz, Yasmine. "Pope Francis Quotes On The Poor" *The Huffington Post,* U.S. edition, August 19, 2013. http://www.huffingtonpost.com/2013/08/19/pope-francis-quotes-poor_n_3780816.html (accessed March 19, 2014).

"Hunger Facts," *Share Our Strength*, http://nokidhungry2.org/hunger-facts (accessed March 16, 2014).

Little, Deborah W. 2004. "Theology of the poor." In *Handbook of U.S. theologies of liberation*, 274-280. St Louis: Chalice Pr, 2004. *ATLA Religion Database with ATLASerials*, EBSCO*host* (accessed January 27, 2014).

McGovern, George, Bob Doyle, Donald E. Messer. *Ending Hunger Now: A Challenge to Persons of Faith.* Minneapolis: Fortress Press, 2005.

Moll, Rob, and Roger Thurow. 2010. "'Hunger can be conquered': and, says former Wall Street Journal reporter Roger Thurow, churches have a crucial role to play." *Christianity Today* 54, no. 2: 40-42. *ATLA Religion Database with ATLASerials*, EBSCO*host* (accessed February 15, 2014).

Morgan, Timothy C., and Isabel Apawo Phiri. 2008. "Hunger isn't history: the world produces more than ever. So why do nearly a billion people still not have enough to eat?." *Christianity Today* 52, no. 11: 26-33. *ATLA Religion Database with ATLASerials*, EBSCO*host* (accessed February 15, 2014).

Murvar, Vatro. 1975. "Toward a sociological theory of religious movements." *Journal For The Scientific Study Of Religion* 14, no. 3: 229-256. *ATLA Religion Database with ATLASerials*, EBSCO*host* (accessed March 18, 2014).

"Progress on Poverty, But 1.2 Billion Still Live on the Extremes." *America* 209, no. 12: 8-9. *Religion and Philosophy Collection*, EBSCO*host* (accessed March 23, 2014).

Robson, Michael. *St. Francis of Assisi: The Legend and the Life.* New York: Wellington House, 1997.

Schatzlein, Joanne. "Francis of Assisi 1181-1220: Christian History Timeline," *Christian History* Issue 42 (1994), http://www.christianitytoday.com/ch/1994/issue42/4226.html (accessed March 21, 2014).

United States Department of Agriculture. Last modified September 4, 2013. Accessed March 16, 2014. http://www.ers.usda.gov/topics/food-nutrition-assistance/food-security-in-the-us/key-statistics-graphics.aspx.http://feedingamerica.org/hunger-in-america/hunger-facts/hunger-and-poverty-statistics.aspx

"U.S. hunger rate still at historic high." *Christian Century,* 2010. 127, no. 25: 17. *ATLA Religion Database with ATLASerials,* EBSCO*host* (accessed February 15, 2014).

Webster, Jill R. 2004. "The poverty of riches: St. Francis of Assisi reconsidered." *Church History* 73, no. 4: 842. *ATLA Religion Database with ATLASerials,* EBSCO*host* (accessed February 15, 2014).

Wheaton, Charles E. 2007. "Blessed are those who hunger." *Living Pulpit* 16, no. 1: 10-12. *ATLA Religion Database with ATLASerials,* EBSCO*host* (accessed February 15, 2014).

Printed in the United States
By Bookmasters